BEYOND THE WORDS
REFLECTIONS ON I AM AFFIRMATIONS

PETER MULRANEY

Copyright © 2018 by Peter Mulraney

All rights reserved.

No part of this book may be reproduced in any form or by any electronic or mechanical means, including information storage and retrieval systems, without written permission from the author, except for the use of brief quotations in a book review.

ISBN: 978-0-6482523-8-2

❧ Created with Vellum

CONTENTS

Introduction	vii
A miracle	1
Amazing	3
Assertive	5
Attentive	7
Attractive	9
Authentic	11
Beautiful	13
Blessed	15
Brilliant	17
Caring	19
Compassionate	21
Complete	23
Confident	25
Courageous	27
Creative	29
Curious	31
Decisive	33
Divine	35
Energetic	37
Enthusiastic	39
Eternal	41
Exciting	43
Free	45
Friendly	47
Funny	49
Generous	51
Genuine	53
Gracious	55
Grateful	57
Happy	59
Healthy	61

Helpful	63
Here	65
Holy	67
Honest	69
Imaginative	71
Incredible	73
Innovative	75
Inspirational	77
Intelligent	79
Intuitive	81
Inventive	83
Jovial	85
Joyful	87
Kind	89
Lovable	91
Loved	93
Loving	95
Mindful	97
Motivated	99
Nurturing	101
One with source	103
Open	105
Optimistic	107
Peaceful	109
Perfect	111
Playful	113
Poised	115
Positive	117
Powerful	119
Productive	121
Prosperous	123
Refreshing	125
Relaxed	127
Sacred	129
Safe	131
Spirit	133
Splendid	135
Spontaneous	137

Successful	139
Supportive	141
Thankful	143
The light	145
Thriving	147
Trusting	149
Valuable	151
Valued	153
Vibrant	155
Welcoming	157
Well	159
Willing	161
A note from Peter	165
Also by Peter Mulraney	167

INTRODUCTION

In *I Am Affirmations: The Power of Words*, I share eighty one positive I am statements that I use as affirmations.

Those affirmations can be used many ways. You can repeat them to yourself, write them out, or read them silently every morning. There are no strict rules.

I hope those affirmations inspire you to write your own as you decide who you want to be and how you want to feel.

When you work with affirmations, it's not uncommon for your negative beliefs to rise to the surface of your awareness in opposition to the positive statements you are now using to describe yourself. You may even hear your ego voice challenging those affirmations. Don't let that discourage you. It means the affirmations are working.

Affirmations are a useful tool for flushing out our negative beliefs about ourselves for examination.

The secret is to stop saying those negative things about yourself once you're aware of them, and letting them go without berating yourself when you become aware of falling back into your old habits. Be kind to yourself.

Consciously using positive I am statements will allow you to think about yourself differently - if you persist.

To succeed, you need to make it a habit that replaces your old habit of talking about yourself negatively, and that requires commitment and self-discipline. But, you're worth it.

It's one thing to use the affirmations.

It's something else again to really think about what each affirmation means to you.

We all use words differently. Each word has a meaning for us within the context of our lives. Sometimes we share a common understanding of what a word means but other times we don't. That's one reason we have dictionaries.

In **Beyond the Words: Reflections on I Am Affirmations**, I explore what the words in the affirmations mean to me.

I hope you find the reflections useful for developing your own understanding of what the words mean for you.

The Biblical references in the text refer to the English Standard Version (ESV).

A MIRACLE

I wake up in the morning. How does that happen? Where was I when I was asleep?

What triggers my return to conscious awareness of my body and surroundings?

When I awake from my slumber, I have a sense of being alive. What keeps me functioning?

Am I breathing?

Or is some presence breathing me?

I'm present in the physical world through a seemingly solid body that scientists are now telling me is composed primarily of nothing - both my body and the physical world are apparently swirling vibrations of energy.

How does that work? How do I maintain the illusion of being a solid form in the physical world?

I have self-awareness but I have no recollection of who or where I was before I came here.

I've defined myself with stories but I know I'm not my stories.

I am a mystery to myself.

I am a miracle.

AMAZING

I am self-aware. Otherwise I'd never know how amazing I am.

I look around, notice things, and wonder about them.

I give everything in my environment a meaning so that it makes sense to me.

I have a body I can move by deciding I want to be somewhere else or to perform a particular task.

I have no idea how those messages move instantaneously from my mind to my limbs. But they do, and I'm able to move my body from one location to another or to persuade parts of it to perform selected actions.

I can shift my centre of attention without moving my body simply by thinking about another place or time. Time travelling inside my mind. Amazing.

I think a thought and move my fingers and words appear on the screen or page, depending on the tool I choose to use.

I think a thought, open my mouth and automatically (without conscious awareness) vibrate my vocal cords and make sounds to communicate with others.

And, I can interpret the sounds made by others.

Amazing.

ASSERTIVE

I struggle with this one. Maybe it's all that good Catholic education about being polite and considering the needs of others or maybe it's simply not understanding what being assertive means.

Being assertive is not about being aggressive. It's about standing up for myself.

Until recently, I was under the misunderstanding that being assertive was being able to say no when I didn't want to do something, but it's much more than that.

Thanks to a story in *Shift Happens* by Robert Holden, I now understand that's only one side of the equation.

Being assertive is also about being able to say yes to opportunities I want to pursue.

It's about standing my ground when someone tries to take advantage of me.

It's about having and expressing a preference.

I know that not being assertive in appropriate circumstances is fear operating.

That fear of being seen as aggressive or selfish or self-promoting. That fear of being the *tall poppy* - the one that's going to be lopped by the crowd. That fear of being laughed at or ignored.

I'm still working with this one, but each day I'm getting closer to knowing: I am assertive.

ATTENTIVE

This one has multiple meanings, depending on the context in which I use it.

I am attentive to detail, which is an important skill in the writing world. I think I can say that's one I have under the belt. Being attentive in that sense is essential to completing any task.

I know about applying attention to what I'm doing but that is only one dimension of being attentive.

What does it mean to say I am attentive?

Is it about paying attention to others?

Now, that sounds like more of a challenge.

How well do I listen when someone else is talking?

How well do I read their non-verbal communication signals?

Being attentive in that sense means choosing to focus on the other, and giving that person my undivided attention.

This might be the one to work on.

ATTRACTIVE

It's tempting to think this means *I am good looking* - but that's only the ego's way of reading it.

I am attractive means I draw things to me. I attract people and events into my life through my beliefs.

This affirmation is a reminder that I'm like a magnet and I need to be aware of my thoughts and beliefs.

My current circumstances are the outcome of my beliefs.

If I'm not happy with my circumstances, there is no point in complaining - I'm the one that attracted them to me.

If I want to change my world, I need to change my beliefs about the world I want to live in so I can attract what I want.

This is a reminder to be awake at all times.

If I fall back into my old thought patterns, I'll be attracting the things I no longer want in my life.

I am attractive and there appears to be no escape from the Law of Attraction.

That's motivation enough to wake up and exercise the power of choice available to me, isn't it?

AUTHENTIC

This is another way of saying I am vulnerable. I am willing to let you see me as I am.

Being authentic means stepping out from behind my mask or persona.

It means putting down my shield and all my weapons and standing unarmed before you.

When I am authentic, what you see is me.

Sounds easy.

But, how often have I stood my ground as myself instead of as whatever role I was playing at the time? And, let's be honest. It's easy to stay behind the facade of a role and be father, husband, lover, friend, cousin and so on instead of just being me.

The challenge is recognising all those thoughts and beliefs I incorporate into my roles and hide behind, and letting them dissolve.

I am not my story or the story of my roles.

I am a soul, and that's what you see when I am authentic.

BEAUTIFUL

I am aware of the reminder Jeshua gives in *The Way of Knowing* to **look at the content and not the form**, when I ponder this affirmation.

The focus is not on the body.

It's on the essence of my being which is, and always shall be, beautiful.

It doesn't matter whether my external appearance measures up to some arbitrary standard of beauty in the world's eyes.

That concept of beauty is false. It's an assessment of packaging or form and misses the point. It's the same as judging a book by its cover and not the story it tells.

This affirmation is a reminder to reclaim my beauty and to let it shine.

It's a reminder to look for the beauty in others, to get to know who they are and not to judge them on appearance alone.

Beauty is not a gift restricted to me nor is it something I need to guard jealously. It can't be taken away from me, so there is no need to hide it.

Beauty is for sharing and enjoying.

BLESSED

This one is a reminder for those days when the voices of the world are filled with gloom and doom.

It's so easy to take all the good things in my life for granted. Things like a lover, a comfortable dwelling, clean air, running water, flushing toilets, good healthy food and a steady stream of income.

How often do I assume my talents and my health will last forever?

I am surrounded by friends that support and encourage me. They are all blessings.

And, what about all those opportunities available to me?

My life is filled with blessings - gifts from my Creator.

It only takes a moment to reflect and appreciate that truth, and that's why I use this affirmation.

BRILLIANT

*B*rilliant! The ego likes this one. It wants it to mean I am exceptionally clever - a genius, in fact. And, on one level, it's probably correct but not for the reasons it thinks.

I am brilliant when I let my light shine - the light of my soul.

That light seeps out through my smile and the twinkle in my eyes. It infuses the electromagnetic field generated by the continuous beating of my heart which announces my presence and broadcasts my intent.

I am brilliant when my mind is open and I listen with my heart and not my ears.

I am brilliant when I shed all of my masks and let my true self be seen.

I am brilliant when I am authentic, when I remember I am spirit, and stop pretending to be someone or something else.

CARING

I care about people. Life is all about relationships with other people.

I care about my body. I want it to keep working while I'm here on the planet, and I have no intention of leaving any time soon.

I care about why I'm here and what I'm doing.

I care about the planet and the way we treat each other.

I care about a lot of things.

I don't understand not caring, even when I see it.

Perhaps it's that Catholic social justice training I received growing up.

Perhaps it's the growing awareness that we are all connected - that we are all one.

There is a danger in caring too much, and it's possible to develop an unhealthy level of caring that leads to worrying about things that I have no influence over, that are not my responsibility.

I am caring and that includes taking care of myself - which may mean letting go of some of my concerns.

COMPASSIONATE

𝒞ompassionate - feeling or showing sympathy and concern for the suffering or misfortune of others.

I admit that I find this one is a bit of a challenge.

I'd like to believe I am compassionate but I know this is often more aspirational than fact.

Sometimes, it's easy to show concern for the suffering or misfortune of others and be moved to action.

At other times, it's more of a challenge, especially when the misfortune appears to be self-inflicted.

Judgement can be a terrible barrier to compassion, even to feeling compassion for myself.

Compassion is love in action.

It's not interfering in other people's lives out of a sense of duty.

Compassion may involve lending a hand, holding space while another heals, or listening to someone's story.

It is not stepping in to save them or fix their problems for them - that's like ripping the butterfly out of its chrysalis before it's ready.

Being compassionate means I support others on their journey to accepting responsibility, while allowing them to learn from their experiences.

I am compassionate is a useful daily reminder that I am not there yet.

COMPLETE

I am complete. It's not me I'm working on but the expression of myself in the world.

It's what I see as my life's work that needs completion.

I was complete when I arrived.

Now, I'm allowing the unfolding of who I am.

I am allowing myself to become visible - all of me and not just the parts I think others might like.

I am removing the parts I've added on, the parts I hide behind, so that I am me and not me making out I am some flawed creation evolving towards completion.

There are no courses I need to complete to be me.

CONFIDENT

*I*t's so easy to hide behind the belief that I am not confident enough.

It's a convenient excuse for not trying new things, for not accepting responsibility, and for leaving it to others to get things done.

When I feel confident, I know I can handle anything.

When I feel confident, I'll give anything a go.

When I feel confident, I'll say hello.

Being confident is no more than believing in myself and my abilities.

Being confident is the key that opens many doors, especially the door only I can open from the inside - the one I hide behind.

Being confident is what allows me to engage with life and to reach out and form relationships with others.

I am confident. I choose to believe in myself.

COURAGEOUS

What is courage?

A willingness to face fears.

I know it takes courage to admit my fears, even to myself, and it takes courage to act when fears seem real.

But acting with courage is what allows me to discover that my fears are not real after all - especially those fears from within that are rooted in beliefs and misinformed thoughts.

Sometimes, courage is listening to my fears and acting with discretion, instead of rushing in fuelled by false bravado and making a costly mistake. Discretion allows me to live to fight another day.

In that respect, courage is a form of wisdom mixed with a belief in my ability to choose the appropriate action in any circumstance.

Courage is the strength that allows me to live by my convictions.

It takes courage to step out from the safety of the herd.

It takes courage to question beliefs that have been handed down for generations or written in so-called sacred texts.

And, those actions are required to wake from the dream and remember who I am.

CREATIVE

I am comfortable with this affirmation. I know I am a creative person.

Before I started writing, I was drawing and making art for my own pleasure.

I enjoy playing with digital images.

In the workplace, I was always the one looking for creative solutions or better ways to do things.

I've designed and planted gardens.

I've made up a million excuses for not doing things and invented fears I let myself believe were true.

It's easy to fall into the trap of thinking creativity only applies to artists or inventors. That's not true.

Anyone who works with their mind is creative.

Anyone who works with their hands is creative.

It's not a talent reserved for special people - we all work with our minds and our hands.

We all start out as creatives. We have imaginary friends, we play make believe, and tell outrageous stories.

Then we go to school and learn to conform and stay between the lines.

We often stifle our creativity in the name of practical reality, forgetting everything practical and functional came from someone's creativity.

Fortunately, no-one can beat your creativity out of you.

They might force you to hide it or to decide you're not creative - until you take this affirmation to heart.

CURIOUS

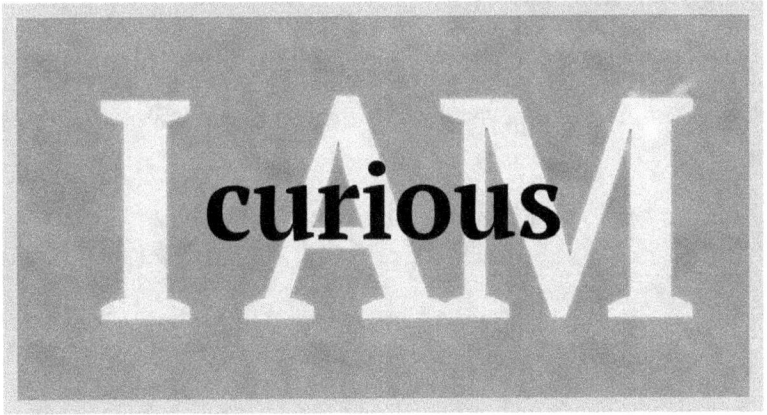

*C*uriosity is a driving force of nature I am very familiar with.

As a small boy, I pulled things apart to find out how they worked.

I know I am not alone in that regard. There are people pulling things apart for precisely that purpose all over the world today, wondering how they were made and what makes them work.

As a parent, I remember my own children asking: Why? How does that work? What is that? What does it do? And all those other questions children ask in their attempts to make sense of the world.

The curious are never satisfied with the status quo. They're interested in how and why things happen and finding new ways of doing things.

The curious drive progress and investigate the power games of the ruling elites.

The curious wonder why people believe what they do, and why they believe things simply because they were written down thousands of years ago or passed along in the oral tradition of story telling and family histories.

I suspect we're all curious.

If we weren't, we'd never do anything different, have adventures or meet new people.

I can't imagine what it must be like to not be curious.

DECISIVE

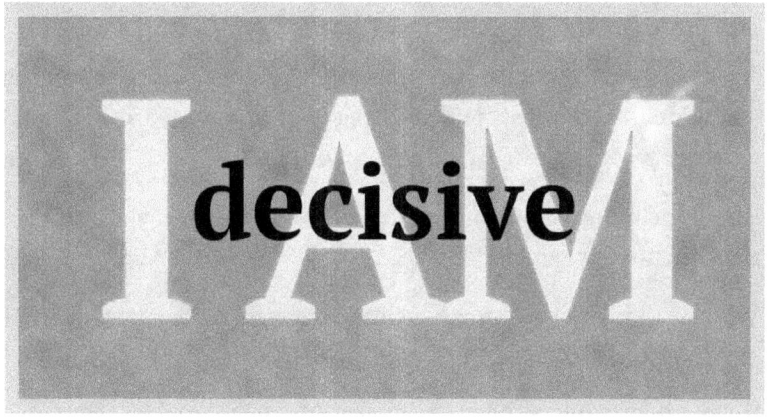

*D*ecisive: to make decisions quickly and effectively.

In some aspects of my life, this is a true statement. In others, it's still aspirational.

The challenge with decisions is living with the consequences.

If decisions and their consequences are minor in nature, it's easy to be decisive. But it's not always so easy when it's a major decision.

The decision to buy a new shirt is not quite the same as the decision to buy a new car.

The decision to ask someone to marry you is not quite the same as asking that same person out on a date.

Some decisions have short-term consequences: no shirt lasts forever and that first date comes to an end no matter how enjoyable or embarrassing.

Others have long-term consequences: you're stuck with that car until you can afford a new one and we still go into marriage expecting it to last forever.

I like to consider all the angles when making an important decision but I still have to make a decision in the end.

Being decisive when you have all the information, and you're acting in your own interest, means making a decision and then acting on it, and not second guessing yourself and worrying about whether you made the right decision or not.

The good thing about many of the decisions we make in life is they are not permanent.

We can change our minds when we get new information or our circumstances change.

When that happens, being decisive means letting go of the previous decision and making a new one.

DIVINE

Nobody believes this one the first time.

The message I heard when I was growing up was that I was a sinner. So how could I possibly be divine?

Misinformation is the short answer.

Somewhere along the line the concept of original sin was introduced into the narrative, despite the Genesis story telling us that God created us in his image.

That would make us divine, wouldn't it?

It's right there at the start of the story. So, what happened?

I forgot. I got so caught up in the game of being in the physical dimension that I came to believe I was a mere mortal - a being with a beginning and an end.

I thought I was the clay of the vessel and forgot about being the breath of God that gives life to the vessel.

Now I know differently.

The vessel returns to the earth but I am the essence of life, and that makes me divine.

ENERGETIC

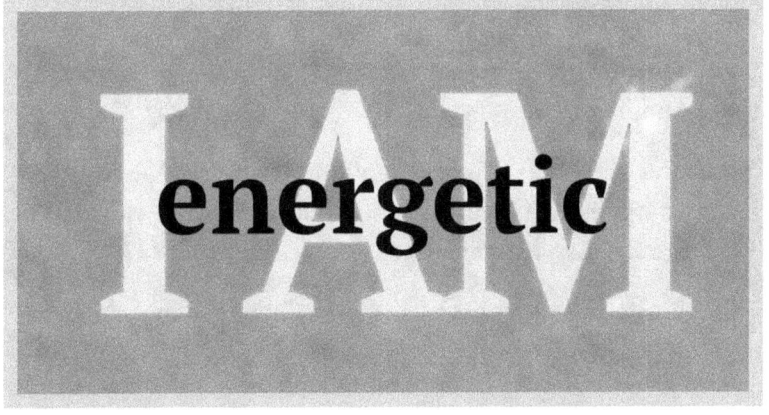

These days, thanks to quantum physics, we know everything in the universe is energy playing as waves and particles at the same time.

That makes me energy.

What makes me appear as a solid body and not a flashing ball of light is the frequency of my vibration.

I wonder if I can increase that frequency to the point where I'd become invisible.

I wonder how many invisible entities there are vibrating right here next to me, outside the range of my awareness antenna.

I am an energy field that spreads out from the centre of my being and influences every thing I encounter.

I wonder if that means I'm being influenced by energy fields I am not consciously aware of, and guided by unseen friends from other dimensions.

Some days, I am aware of other energy fields.

Some of those fields feel uplifting.

Others feel as though they are draining my battery.

I wonder how others perceive my field, even when my intention is to be uplifting.

No matter what my frequency of vibration, one of the realities of being energy is that I am always vibrating and broadcasting my signature signal to the universe.

Something else to be conscious of as I go about my business.

ENTHUSIASTIC

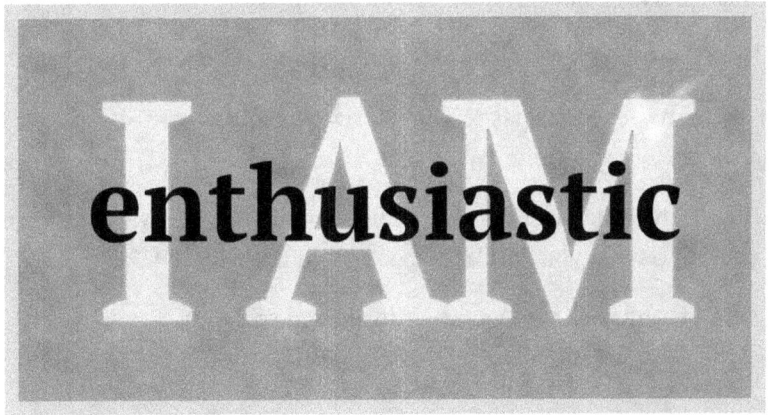

*E*nthusiasm can get you into trouble, especially if you let your enthusiasm for something get the better of you, and you rush into action before considering all the consequences of your decisions.

One of the things I had to be aware of in my project management activities in the workplace was rushing into solution mode before I understood the problem.

Sometimes, you have to put your enthusiasm on a leash and develop a project plan.

But, there is a place for enthusiasm.

I like to bring my enthusiasm to those things I'm passionate about; those things I want to do.

Sitting down to write day after day is a lot easier when you're enthusiastic about what you're doing.

It's not so much fun if you only see what you're doing as a task you have to complete.

In fact, I suspect doing anything day after day is a lot easier when you bring enthusiasm to the table. I know it was for me when I was working in jobs that weren't exciting every day.

Enthusiasm isn't restricted to work.

You can be enthusiastic about relationships, causes, sporting activities, or anything.

Being enthusiastic is really about bringing your attention and energy to what you're doing and who you're with.

Being enthusiastic is enjoying the life you're living.

ETERNAL

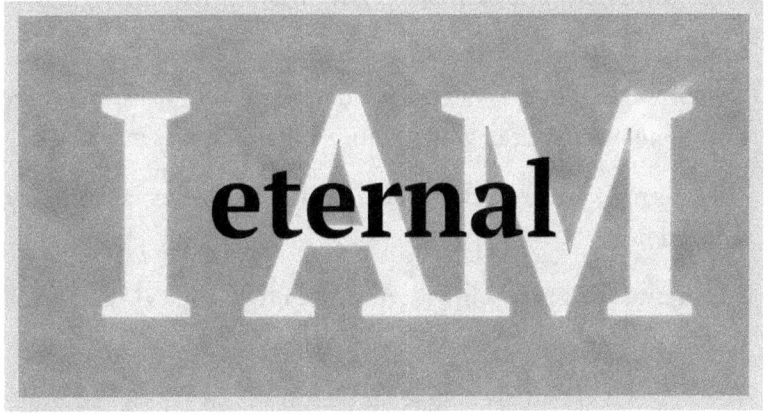

Who is the I this applies to? It can't be Peter. He is a personality and we all know Peter is going to die. Even I know that. And, that means Peter is not eternal in any sense of the word.

If I want to acknowledge this affirmation as true, I need to acknowledge that I am not Peter.

I am something else, something beyond the realm of three-dimensional physical reality.

If I am eternal, then I am divine.

To take this as truth, I must accept myself as being spirit, soul, or pure awareness without form.

I can't hold onto any idea of being only human or a body. The body and personality are simply the forms I've elected to take in order to appear here in this realm.

This dimension may not be the only realm of existence. But, it could be.

It could have realms, not discernible through the senses of the body, which allow the eternal to exist invisible to us but right here beside us.

Perhaps God is always watching and looking out for us, and there really is no place we can go without being in the presence of God.

I am eternal and so is everyone else. It's not a special category. We're all in it.

This lifetime will pass - and it's not the only one I have had or will have.

When Peter has run his course and left his legacy, I will continue to exist and simply return my attention to the place where my soul always is, eternally.

EXCITING

There are days when I think my life is fairly routine with nothing to write home about.

Sometimes, it's hard to get excited about how things are. But that's not what this affirmation is about.

I am exciting.

Being me is exciting.

The important question is not whether other people find me exciting or not. The question is: am I exciting to myself?

It would be easy to think I'm just another insignificant being roaming the face of the earth. Nothing special. Nothing to get excited about.

But, I am unique.

There is no-one else exactly like me.

There is no-one else walking my path, having my experiences, and receiving my insights.

No-one sees anything exactly the way I do.

No-one sees the same possibilities, the same connections, or makes the same discoveries.

No-one relates to others the way I do.

No-one expresses themselves the way I express myself.

Everything in life is a question of perspective and my perspective is my unique view of life.

No-one else is being me, and being me is exciting.

FREE

The only chains that bind me are the ones I attach myself.

And, those chains are nothing but thoughts or beliefs.

I am free to change my mind about any of them.

I am not bound by social conventions or other people's expectations unless I choose to be - and I am free to choose.

I am free to believe whatever I think is true.

I am not obliged to align my beliefs with any doctrine or ideology - but I am free to do so.

I am free to choose how I will behave.

I am free to choose how I will respond to other people.

I am free to play by the rules of society or to ignore them.

I am free to choose my own rules and march to the beat of my own drum.

I am not the body.

I am spirit, and spirit is always free - even from death.

FRIENDLY

𝓘 enjoy being with people.

I like discussing ideas with friends and meeting new people.

I'm not interested in creating conflict.

I see being friendly as a disposition, a way of being open to others.

It's a way of relating to people in general, of treating people with respect and acknowledging their inherent dignity.

Being friendly costs nothing and often works wonders.

People appreciate being treated with respect, especially when they're doing their best to serve me in difficult situations.

Being friendly makes it easy to help the people that ask for directions when I'm walking about the city.

Being friendly is an enjoyable experience - and it is often contagious.

I am friendly by nature and by choice.

FUNNY

I can get people to laugh and I laugh at myself.

I see humour as a great gift and I enjoy inserting it into social interactions.

Not only is laughter good medicine, it's also a great ice breaker, and being able to be funny is often a blessing.

But funny has another meaning - being difficult to explain or strange - and, maybe that's true of me too.

Anybody who steps outside of the herd's mentality and starts asking questions about what the group believes to be true has to be a little strange.

It's certainly challenging in some groups to explain why I do that, and why I have let go of certain beliefs and worldviews.

Maybe I'm not the only one that's funny in that sense.

GENEROUS

I share. I pass things on. I collaborate. I give my time and resources to support others.

I share my insights and understanding so others can benefit from my learning.

I give others the benefit of the doubt.

I listen when others need an audience to voice their fears and concerns.

I know how to let go of things so others can use them.

I understand that I am a steward and not the owner of the things that come into my possession.

I am here to expand the presence of love.

That requires generosity of spirit.

But, the beauty of giving love is its never ending supply.

The more I give away the more there is.

GENUINE

$\mathcal{S}$aying I am genuine is claiming that I am sincere.

When I am genuine, I'm not putting on an act to please or impress someone.

I do things because I choose to do them.

I help others because I want to help them and not to further my own agenda.

When I am genuine, I am not pretending to listen. I am listening attentively. I'm paying attention to the present moment and noticing the person in front of me.

When I am genuine, I am letting my light shine. I am not hiding behind a mask. I am being myself.

And, when I'm being myself, I am genuine.

GRACIOUS

Being gracious is not one of the ego's attributes. The ego is not magnanimous in any shape or form.

I know, from long experience, that being gracious requires conscious effort to become a lived reality.

Being gracious involves making a choice in how I respond to a situation, especially a situation that has not gone my way.

It's choosing to accept defeat at the hands of an opponent who has played with superior skills on the day, without blaming, or claiming I was robbed by the umpire. And, more importantly, without wanting revenge.

Being gracious is choosing not to offend or intentionally hurt another's feelings.

It involves taking the other person's viewpoint and sensibilities into account when responding.

Being gracious is not taking offence when I could - if I was siding with my ego.

Becoming gracious requires acquiring the skills of diplomacy, and I know that takes patience - the patience of a saint. But that patience is not beyond me.

Being gracious means being awake - so I am aware of what's going on in my presence and can respond in love.

Being gracious is acting under the guidance of love.

GRATEFUL

It is so easy to take life and all its blessings for granted.

It's also easy to focus on the negative and complain when things are not going according to my plan.

So many teachers remind us to be grateful. *Gratitude is the attitude* is a common mantra.

I am grateful for the gift of life. I know I didn't create myself. I am an expression of God's love in form.

If God hadn't thought me into being I wouldn't exist, and if God stops thinking about me I will no longer exist.

I am grateful that God thinks about me constantly.

HAPPY

I am happy. It's a state of being that does not depend on my circumstances.

I can decide to be happy at any time and under any conditions, just as easily as I can decide not to be happy.

It took me a while to figure this one out.

The message of western culture is you can't be happy until something good happens to you or someone loves you or approves of you.

That puts all the power to determine happiness into events I can't control.

When I abide by that message, my life becomes a pursuit of happiness instead of being an experience of happiness.

Awakening involves accepting that I, and I alone, am responsible for my life.

That means taking back all my power, including the power to be happy whenever I choose.

I am happy.

It's a much better state of being than choosing to remain unhappy or to wait for someone or something to make me happy.

HEALTHY

I am healthy in body, mind, and spirit.

Staying healthy takes commitment.

The body requires nutrition, exercise, and sleep. It enjoys movement.

The mind requires stimulation and exposure to new ideas. It enjoys being creative and telling stories. It knows a lot more than the ego, which only thinks it's the mind without knowing that it isn't.

The spirit requires quiet time away from the noise and distractions of the world and the ego. It enjoys solitude and listening to the Holy Spirit, the voice for God, which can only be heard when I meditate and dial down the voice of the ego to zero.

HELPFUL

Being helpful means I'm working for the greater good and not self aggrandizement.

I am not here to lord it over anyone.

My role is that of servant. I am here to help.

Being of service does not mean being someone else's lackey or slave. It means having something to offer and being willing to share so that others may benefit.

Being helpful means lending a hand when others ask for support with completing a task or project.

Being helpful means going with the flow instead of resisting the gifts life is sending my way.

Being helpful means remembering I am a channel and that all good things flow through me.

Being helpful requires being present to the moment I'm in - so I'll recognize the opportunities to be of service that life offers me.

HERE

I am where my attention is focused.

To be in the present moment as a human, I need to focus my attention where my body is: here.

My mind may want to wander off into thoughts of the past down memory lane or into a fantasy of some future world, but I chose to be here.

I chose to incarnate and experience life as a human on this planet.

To get the most of that experience it's obvious that I need to focus my attention where my body is in the present moment.

It's tempting to think that being spiritual is all about the inner journey or that it's all about detaching from the world of form, the world of material things.

But that is not spirituality. It's escapism.

Yes, it's important to maintain an awareness of my connection to Source through prayer and meditation but that is not why I'm here.

I am here to experience being human.

And, to fully experience what it is to be human, I need to engage with life and participate in the human dimension of existence.

If I'm not doing that I'm only observing, and I could have done that without incarnating - but I am here.

HOLY

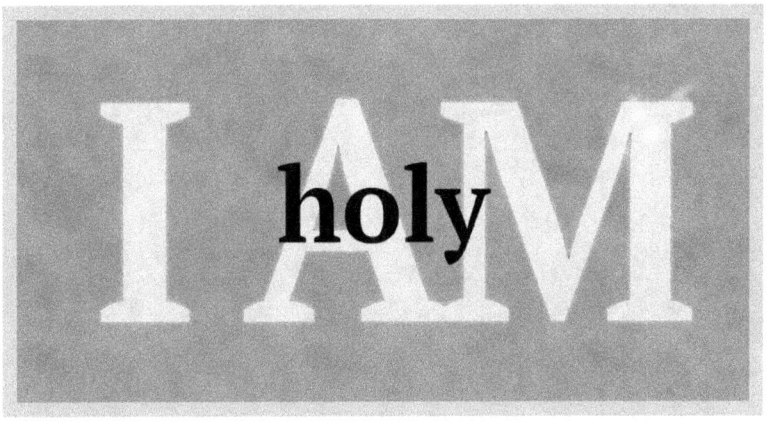

A holy person is someone in the service of God.

Fortunately, I do not need to be a saint to be holy.

What I need is the intent and willingness to act in the service of God.

This can be dangerous, especially if I succumb to the temptation of thinking I know the mind of God, which is an impossibility.

But I can be guided by the Holy Spirit if I am prepared to listen and ask for guidance. That's what prayer is for - asking for guidance and listening for the answer in silence.

A holy person is not called to set up a theocracy and rule in the name of God. That is not acting in the service of God. That is acting as God.

Being in the service of God means expanding the presence of Love wherever I am.

Jesus put it fairly simply - love God, and love your neighbour as you love yourself. (Mark 12:30-31 ESV)

That's all I have to do to be holy.

I can do that.

HONEST

The hardest person to be honest with is myself.

It's way easier to be honest with others. Accountability takes care of that.

Being dishonest requires a conscious decision to act deceitfully or speak an untruth.

Doing those things creates an immediate sense of unease, a knowing that I am not doing the right thing. That's usually enough to keep me honest in my dealings with others.

It might also be the outcome of years of exposure to Catholic teaching on conscience.

But it's easy to lie to myself. It's often convenient to deny the truth, especially a truth I do not want to know about.

In one of the lessons in the *Way of Mastery*, Jeshua says there are no secrets, even if I choose to believe otherwise, and he points out that I only need to pay attention to my thoughts and watch my behaviour to know myself.

An interesting way of saying I can run but I can't hide from myself.

The honest action is to face myself and decide I have nothing to hide.

IMAGINATIVE

I am a storyteller. I make stuff up for entertainment.

I am a problem solver. I dream up creative solutions and new ways of doing things.

I am an artist. I transform thoughts into images.

I am a thinker. I wonder why things are the way they are and why people do the things they do.

I am a time traveller. I go to distant places in my mind.

I am a reader. I go on adventures within the pages of a book.

I am a dreamer. I visualise different realities.

I am imaginative. I use my creative gifts.

INCREDIBLE

I am vast beyond my knowing.

The universe exists within me.

The world is a figment of my imagination.

I am connected to God, the source of my being.

I am connected to the one mind that guides all living beings.

I am animating a body and playing in the realm of time and space, where energy appears as matter.

I am an eternal spirit who has enjoyed many incarnations, many lifetimes.

I am incredible.

Yet, I believe in myself.

INNOVATIVE

One of my childhood mentors was a man named Alf Haines, a farmer with humble origins.

He started out with very little and gradually expanded a drover's small holding into a self-supporting farming enterprise.

Alf's enduring lesson was the one on how to make do with what you had; how to solve a problem with the materials you had on hand when you couldn't afford to purchase someone else's ready-made solution.

It is amazing what some things can be used for - applications their original designers probably never considered possible.

This was my introduction to innovation. It opened the door to my creative approach to fixing things and constructing something to solve any problem I encounter using my available resources.

Sometimes I am successful straight away. The solution is obvious - once I've thought about it and considered what I have available to play with.

Sometimes the solution appears to be beyond my resources. But, with a little patience and a little distance, a solution often pops into my mind.

It comes from believing I am innovative.

INSPIRATIONAL

Being inspirational is part of my life's calling.
It's about allowing others to see that each of us is a lot more than what we think we are.

Being inspirational is about setting an example.

It is about doing the things that others only talk or dream about.

Being inspirational involves stepping into the arena and performing in the public spotlight.

It's about reminding others that life is a field of possibilities and not a pre-determined journey.

You can't do that sitting in the stands watching others play the game. You have to be one of the players on the field.

Inspiring others requires a level of self-belief. You have to believe you have something of value to offer before you'll take the risk of offering it to others.

Being inspirational is an act of courage. It's an act of faith.

It's not always appreciated - but it is essential if others are to awaken to the possibilities life offers.

INTELLIGENT

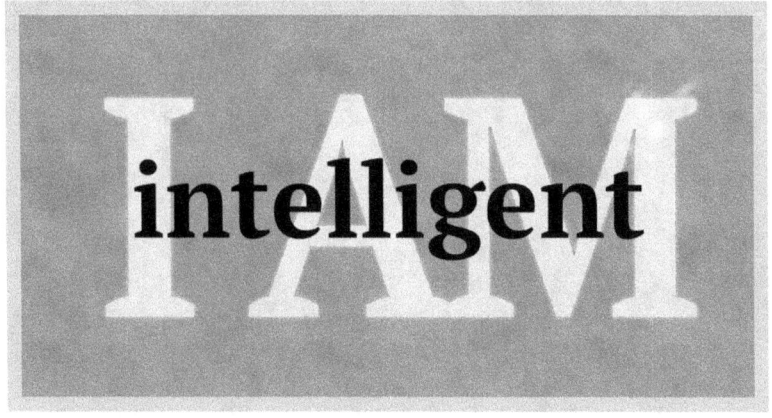

I am intelligent.

I am a sentient being. I have self-awareness. I know I exist.

I know things about myself and my surroundings.

I work things out, solve puzzles, and overcome obstacles using my mind.

I remember things about myself, other people, events, and things in my environment.

I understand the language of my tribe and communicate with those around me using written and spoken words.

I recognize emotional states - mine and those of the people I am with.

I relate to others in non-threatening ways - aware of the impact of my words and actions.

But being intelligent isn't just about being smart.

It's about being awake, considerate, and compassionate.

INTUITIVE

I trust my gut feelings.
I ask for guidance and listen for answers.
Sometimes I simply know.
It wasn't always like this.

I had a rational, scientific education. I was schooled in logical thought. I was taught that knowledge had to be acquired through learning and direct experience.

Now I know differently.

Now I know I exist in an energy field and can tap into universal consciousness where all knowledge exists.

Being intuitive is not a special gift or talent reserved for the privileged few. It's universal. It's always available - but we aren't always open to receiving the message.

Meditation is a doorway to intuition. Step through it.

INVENTIVE

*B*eing inventive is a corollary to being creative and imaginative.

Being inventive is applying thought and skills to transform creative or imaginative ideas into reality.

The creative me thinks of a story idea. The inventive me turns the idea into a book and the story takes on a form of its own - separate from me.

The imaginative me dreams. The inventive me takes the steps required to turn my dreams into my reality.

The creative me visualizes a concept. The inventive me draws a diagram or paints a picture so others can see what I see.

Being inventive allows me to find a way through, around, under, or over obstacles on my path.

I am grateful that inventiveness is a talent available to all, and not reserved for geniuses or super intelligent people.

JOVIAL

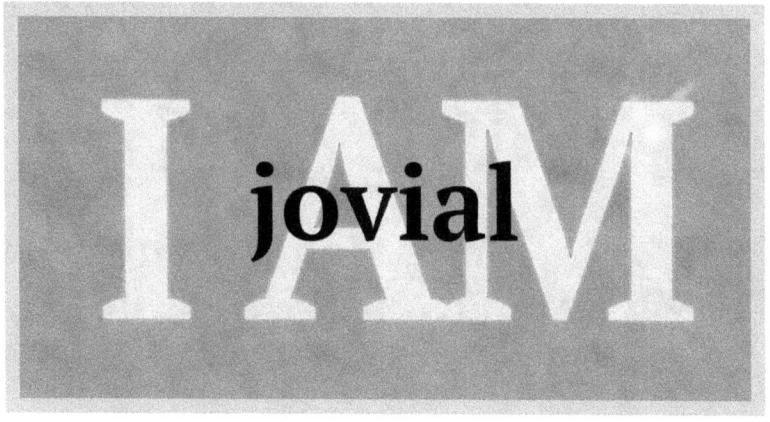

I am jovial.

I am good-humoured.

I am fun loving.

I am cheerful and friendly.

I see the bright side of life.

I don't take myself too seriously.

I can laugh at myself and with you when you're laughing at me.

I like jokes and I'll laugh at yours, too.

I know I'm here to enjoy life and what the world has to offer.

Abraham tells us that life is meant to be fun, so being jovial must mean I'm in alignment.

JOYFUL

I am joyful means I am full of joy, a feeling of great pleasure and happiness.

I know there are times when I don't feel that way, even though I'm aware I can always choose to be joyful.

It is so easy to let the circumstances of life dictate how I feel.

And, there are times when joy does not seem to be the appropriate response, for example, when someone I love dies or is suffering.

In those moments, it seems more appropriate to feel sad or concerned.

There is another way to look at this.

It's the soul that is always full of joy.

When I'm aware of being a soul and not just a personality acting through a body, I can tap into that joy any time I choose, regardless of how I might be feeling about the circumstances of my life.

Joy as the grounding of being, instead of joy as a feeling to express when things are going well for me.

It all comes back to perspective and how I see myself.

I am a soul enjoying every experience, even the ones that don't seem so great from the human point of view.

KIND

*I*sn't it interesting how we are kind to others and not so kind to ourselves?

I suspect it's because we got the *be kind to others* rule drummed into us from an early age.

We were encouraged to share our toys and play nicely with our siblings. When we got to school, there were all those rules governing our behaviour and we got into trouble if we didn't play nice.

I know it didn't take me long to work out how to play the game.

But who teaches you to be kind to yourself?

It's a mistake to think being kind to yourself is being selfish.

Being kind to yourself is an act of love.

It's an act of compassion for the most important person in your life - you.

Give yourself permission to be kind to yourself.

Being kind to others is easy once you make a commitment to be kind to yourself.

LOVABLE

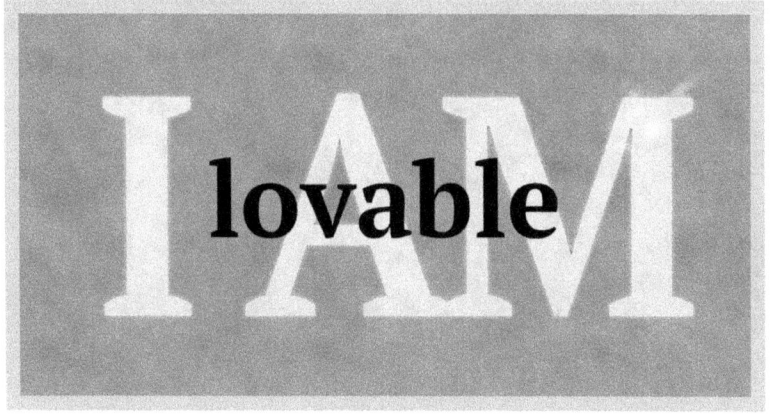

I am lovable.

I am enough.

I am worthy.

There is nothing inherently wrong with me.

I did not come into the world flawed through the stain of some imagined original sin.

I came shining with the light of original blessing.

I am as my creator created me: an expression of Love in form.

~

One of the biggest illusions you can buy into is the idea that you are not lovable, and there are plenty of people who will tell you that you are not lovable - but that is only their misguided opinion and not fact.

You can act as if you believe that you are not lovable, but the only person you are deluding with that belief is yourself.

God always loves you, no matter what. That's how unconditional love works.

If you're still not convinced, find a Bible and read the story of the Prodigal Son. (Luke 15:11-32 ESV)

It's your story.

LOVED

I am loved.

I am accepted for who I am as I am.

There are people in my life that tell me they love me.

I choose to believe them.

I love myself.

I accept myself as I am.

It doesn't matter if some people claim not to love me.

That's their prerogative but it doesn't change the reality of my being loved.

I am always loved by God.

LOVING

This is the third affirmation in a trilogy of affirmations Jeshua presents in the *Way of Mastery*:

- I am lovable,
- I am loved, and
- I am loving.

If my life purpose is to expand the presence of Love in the world of form, there is only one way of being that allows me to do that: being loving.

I am loving. I accept others for who they are. I see them as God sees them: whole and complete.

God does not see the form. God sees the spark of the divine essence within and I am called to do the same.

Not always easy. It's easy to be distracted by the form or the behaviour of the person in front of me.

I am loving is a decision I choose to make every day.

MINDFUL

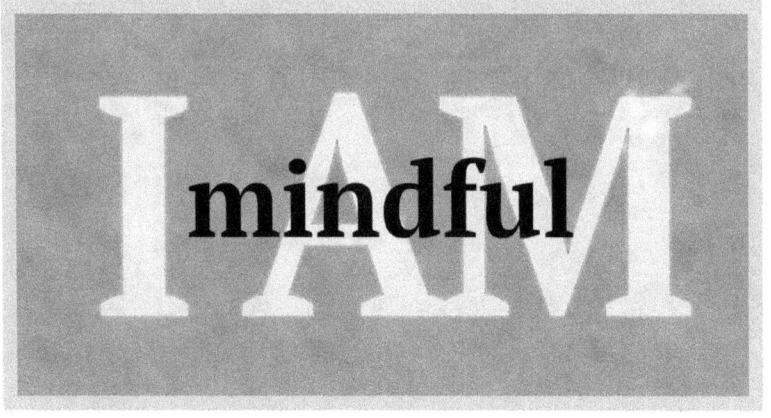

I am mindful.

I keep things in awareness.

I pay attention.

I am in the present moment.

It is not so easy to be present but mindfulness facilitates presence.

Being mindful means keeping my mind where my body is because my attention is focused by the thoughts in my mind.

If I am thinking about something else when you are talking to me, I am not paying attention to you. I'm paying attention to my thoughts.

Being mindful when I am in your presence requires that I put my thoughts aside and give my whole attention to you.

Mindful meditation allows me to choose to give my whole attention to my thoughts or to put my thoughts aside and give my whole attention to the voice for God: the Holy Spirit.

When I choose to pay attention to my thoughts, I uncover what I am thinking and discern my beliefs.

When I choose to pay attention to the voice for God, I hear the guidance of the Holy Spirit.

MOTIVATED

My motivation comes from within.

I do not need an external reason or excuse to do anything.

My actions are connected to my desires.

I am working to achieve my goals.

I am working to fulfil my life purpose.

I have a reason for living, a reason for getting up in the morning, a reason for continuing, and I give myself that reason.

According to *A Course in Miracles*, the choice is always between Love and Fear.

Love motivates from within and encourages expansion.

Fear motivates from without with threats of pain or loss.

I choose to be motivated by the desire to expand the presence of Love in all that I do.

NURTURING

I am nurturing makes me think of gardening.

I know any seeds I plant will have a better chance of survival if I prepare the soil and then water and fertilise them as they grow. And, I'll need to weed the garden and protect those seedlings from the animals that want to eat them.

Nurturing requires attention, commitment, and a liberal application of loving kindness.

But plants aren't the only things I am called to nurture.

My relationships require nurturing. They will not grow and prosper on their own without my engagement.

My life's work requires nurturing. It doesn't happen on its own without my input.

My inner journey requires nurturing. It doesn't happen unless I commit to it and devote the time required to explore the inner realms.

I require nurturing, as an act of self-love to remind myself that I am important to me.

I'm called to nurture others, to plant seeds in their minds and support them on their journey of awakening to self-awareness.

ONE WITH SOURCE

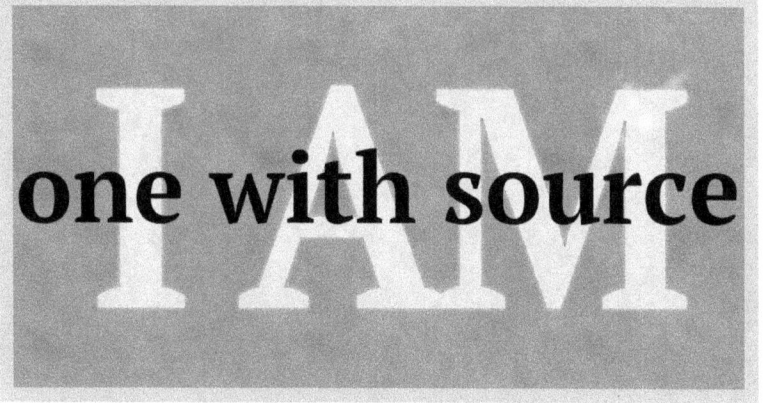

Source is another word for Creator or God.

I am one with my Creator. It is not possible to be otherwise.

I am one with Source.

I am one with God.

Jesus tried to tell us this truth: *I and the Father are one.* (John 10:22 ESV). We didn't want to listen then and it seems we don't want to listen now.

We want to make Jesus a special case. But, there are no special cases. Not even for reputed messiahs.

We are all connected to Source whether we want to acknowledge it or not.

I choose to acknowledge my connection.

I am one with Source.

OPEN

I am open - like a pipe is open. I allow things to flow in, through, and out. I am not hoarding the experiences, ideas, insights, money, people, or things that come into my life.

I am open to learning and teaching.

I am open to exploring new ways and putting aside the old ways of doing things.

I am open to releasing beliefs and practices that no longer serve me.

I am open to questioning what I have been told is the truth.

I am open to forming lasting relationships and letting people move on when the time comes.

I am open to change and exploring new experiences.

I am open to pursuing my dreams and doing the work required to bring them to fruition.

I am open means I choose vulnerability and relinquish my defensive shield.

I am open means I choose to be myself in the world.

I am open means I choose to listen when you speak to me.

OPTIMISTIC

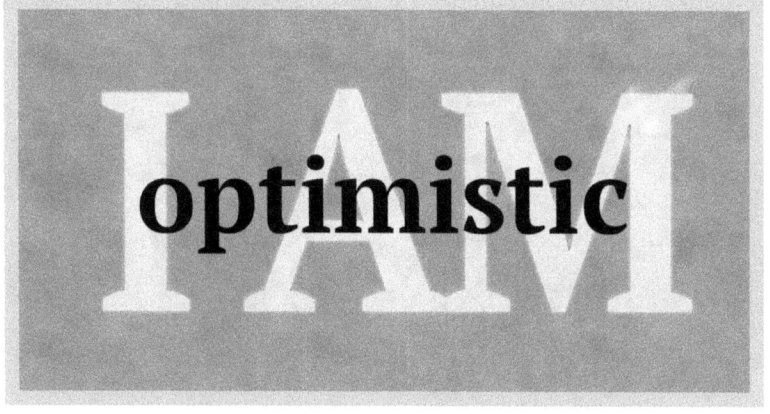

I choose to believe things always work out for the better. I am optimistic.

I see no point in thinking things will not work out.

It hasn't always been like this.

I can recall being lost in worst-case scenario thinking. That was when I was listening to the voice of fear. It was scary stuff, but as I became more mindful, more aware, I realized those worst-case scenarios never happened.

I let them go. I stopped indulging my worst-case scenario fantasies and started looking at the possibilities available to me.

Letting go of my fears was liberating.

I'm not going back to worrying about potential disasters waiting for me in the shadows when I have a more uplifting alternative.

I am optimistic and I've noticed that things work out for the better - every time.

PEACEFUL

I am peaceful, free from disturbance, and tranquil in spirit.

I know this one is aspirational, because there are still moments when I lose my sense of self and forget where I am and that I am connected to God, the source of all peace.

But each day I choose to be at peace regardless of what is going on around or within me.

Each day I choose love over chaos and conflict, because I know peace is the outcome of allowing the miracle of love to flow through me.

Each day I make time to meditate and remind myself that I am connected to Source and that I am always safe.

PERFECT

How often have I chased the dream of perfection, believing I was not good enough?

How often have I let the standard of perfection be the barrier stopping me from taking action?

How often have I confused the standard of my performance or behaviour with my self-worth?

I am an adult now. I don't need to seek approval or evaluate my worth through the judgement by others.

That was the stuff of childhood where I thought my worth depended on what others told me about myself, and often their evaluation was of my behaviour or performance. It wasn't about my self-worth.

I was the one who mistakenly believed their evaluation applied to my self-worth.

There is nothing wrong with me. I am good enough and I have always been good enough, because I am perfect just as I am.

If I put in a not so good performance, it's the performance that's not perfect.

I can work on polishing my skills.

I do not have to work on polishing myself - I am perfect just as I am.

PLAYFUL

𝒯aking myself seriously is a mistake.

I'm playing the game of life and, no matter how carefully I play, I make mistakes. That's how I learn.

Actually, I'm always on a learning curve.

It's okay to take a wrong turn every now and then. It's okay to fumble the ball. It's all in the name of experience, and the fun is in the playing, not in whether I win or lose.

In fact, I can't lose. Life isn't about winning or losing. It's about experience and that involves making decisions, taking risks, and seeing what happens.

Then I get to choose again. No outcome is permanent. Everything is in a state of flux and it's much more fun going with the flow than worrying about getting it wrong.

And, the good thing, about being playful and not taking myself too seriously, is I get to laugh at myself and enjoy the experiences I am having, regardless of their outcomes.

POISED

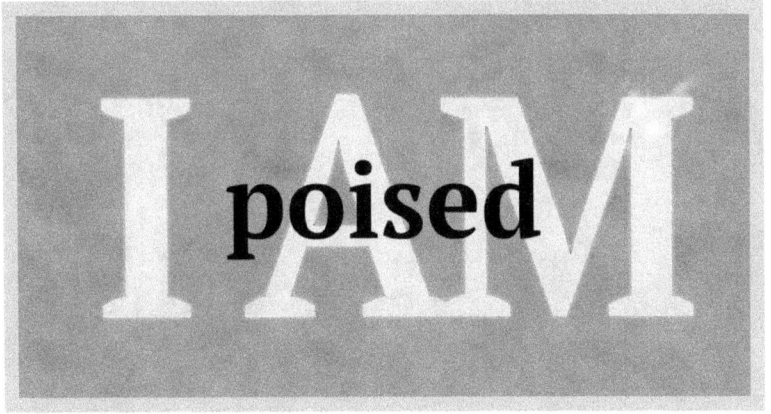

*P*oised: having a composed and self-assured manner.

This is a corollary of being peaceful.

When I am at peace, I feel self-assured.

When I am at peace, I can cope with any circumstance.

It would be great to be poised every waking moment but every now and then I forget, and I lose my composure. I let things get to me and have to remind myself to breathe.

From experience, I now know it's easier to keep my composure when I decide not to take things personally.

When I remind myself that no-one plans their days around attacking me, it's so much easier to remember that any act is either an expression of love or a call for help.

When I am in the presence of Love, I am poised.

POSITIVE

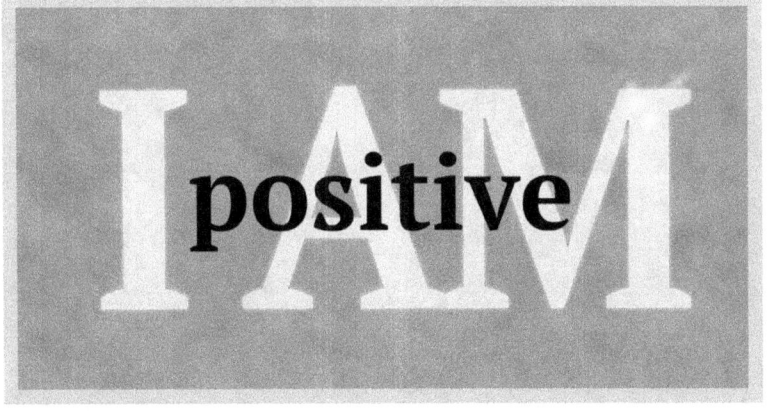

I give my attention to the things I want to happen.

I focus on doing the things I'm good at.

I look for the things that are working.

I look for the good in life - there are more than enough people pointing out the things that are wrong.

I have learnt to reframe the negative. All events are neutral and it's only my interpretation that makes them good or bad for me.

I'm always looking for the silver lining within the storm clouds.

I choose to see obstacles or disasters as opportunities.

Yes, they may stop my progress temporarily or redirect my efforts, but they always yield their gifts when I stop complaining and look for the reason behind them.

Even endings are positive, since every ending opens up the possibility of a new beginning.

I choose to be positive.

POWERFUL

I am the creator of my own reality.

I'm doing it all day every day through my thoughts and beliefs.

For the first part of my life, I was blissfully unaware I was attracting experiences aligned with my thoughts.

Then I studied *A Course in Miracles* and the *Way of Mastery*, read about the Law of Attraction, and realized I was responsible for my life.

Now, if I want to know what I have consciously or subconsciously chosen to believe, all I have to do is look at the circumstances of my life.

Fortunately, as Jeshua says frequently in the *Way of Mastery*, if I am not enjoying my current experience I can change my mind and create a new one.

I am not the victim of my circumstances. I am their creator.

Acknowledging I am powerful is an essential step in the process of taking responsibility for my life.

PRODUCTIVE

This is a good one for those days when it seems I haven't achieved anything. For those days when I've been busy all day and have nothing to show for it.

It's important to remember that I am productive is a statement about my long-term performance as much as it is a statement about today's.

One way to remind myself of how productive I am is to review my list of accomplishments; those things I have produced that I believe represent my contribution.

I am productive is a mindset I take into any work situation, and I know from long experience that thinking that way allows me to be productive.

Being productive is a choice and it doesn't always mean working non-stop.

Sometimes, the most productive thing is to sit and contemplate, and not rush to get the job done.

PROSPEROUS

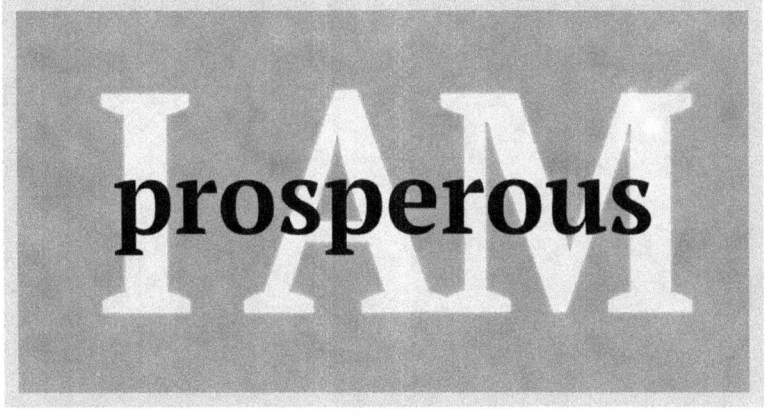

*P*rosperous - successful in material terms; flourishing financially. Well, that's what the dictionary claims.

Being prosperous is more about my mindset, how I see myself in the world, and not so much about my bank account balance.

When I see myself as prosperous, it's much easier to be generous, not only in terms of money but in sharing anything I have, including time, knowledge and ideas.

It's a good feeling having access to the money required to fund my preferred lifestyle choices. And, it feels great being in a position to help others, knowing that doing so is not really diminishing the supply of the good things that prosperity brings.

One of the temptations associated with being prosperous is hoarding or keeping all the good stuff for myself.

But, if I'm honest with myself, I know that hoarding is a sign I've succumbed to the fear of scarcity, the belief that there isn't enough to go around.

That's hardly an attitude congruent with being prosperous.

REFRESHING

I am being made new again. This is a meaning that's come to me from the world of computers.

It seems every other day there's an update to refresh the operating system or one of the programs on my computer.

If I open the web browser, there's a button to click for refreshing the webpage I'm viewing in case it's changed since the last time I looked at it.

Meditation is one way I use for refreshing my operating system.

Reading is a way of updating my programs by refreshing my beliefs.

If I do not engage in refreshing activities I remain the same. I go stale.

Unless I refresh, I continue to operate on outdated beliefs.

I am refreshing.

It's a commitment.

And, when I keep that commitment, I am refreshing to be with.

RELAXED

I have given up being stressed out.

I know stress has its good points in some situations - but only in moderation.

I've learnt that excessive stress is not good for me or those around me.

Excessive stress leads to panic, mistakes, and unnecessary conflict. I can do without those.

Everything works so much better when I am relaxed - even if others around me are stressed.

I prefer to relax and go with the flow instead of trying to swim upstream against the current.

Not trusting the flow is where all my stress comes from, and it's so exhausting fighting life as it's happening. I'd rather keep my energy for living.

I am relaxed does not mean I am asleep.

It means I've learnt to trust life - even when things do not appear to be working out.

SACRED

*M*ost people could make a list of what is regarded as sacred.

We have sacred places, sacred objects, sacred texts, and sacred ideas.

If we think of people as sacred, we call them saints and think they are so unlike us.

We have been taught to regard ourselves as sinners, those that need salvation.

But, the truth is, we are the children of God.

That makes every one of us sacred.

We treat all those things we regard as sacred with reverence.

I am sacred.

How much reverence am I showing for myself?

SAFE

I am safe. I am not likely to be harmed. I am protected.

Safety is an interesting concept. What do I need to feel safe from? Who wants to hurt me?

There are plenty of voices telling me that I live in an unsafe world but my experience does not align with their opinion.

Where does all that fear come from?

If I let go of my fears, I feel safe. I can relax in the knowledge that no-one is out to harm me. The universe is a safe place, especially when I see it's all within me.

I am safe. I am not likely to harm anyone.

This is another way of reading the words.

I am a presence of love in the world and love wouldn't hurt anyone, would it?

But love can be a disturbing presence that is often seen as unsafe by those unfamiliar with it. Loving calls for trust and for letting go of outcomes, and it risks being ignored.

But the beauty of self-love is knowing I am safe.

My very sense of being safe within myself is a challenge to those that see the world as an unsafe and scary place.

Fear is afraid of love.

The ego is afraid of love. If it has nothing to protect me from, it thinks it has no role to play until it learns it exists to serve and not to lead.

Then, we both know that I am safe.

SPIRIT

This means I am non-physical.

Part of me does not believe this. That part wants me to believe I am a body and separate from everything else in the universe.

When I listen to that part, I feel lonely and afraid. I feel insignificant - a tiny dot of protoplasm, standing on a small planet orbiting a star in a galaxy far from the centre of the known universe.

Spirit is not something I can see, but it's something I feel when I meditate and seem to be somewhere else, beyond the confines of the body.

In the *Way of Mastery*, Jeshua says it's what I remember being when I release my attachments to the physical world and my belief in being separate. Meditation is the closest I get to that, I suppose.

In reality, spirit is living as me here. That's the meaning of incarnation, a spirit merging with a body to engage with life in the physical dimension.

I am not meant to forget that I have a body. A body is an essential tool for experiencing life here.

Awakening is simply remembering that I am more than a body and that when the body expires I will continue, as I always have.

SPLENDID

I am splendid.

I am magnificent.

Just like everybody else.

It's not the little me that I present to others that is splendid. That's my human form, my avatar, through which I am present in the world.

When I focus on being in the world, I see myself as a human. I have a personality and a range of eccentricities that make me unique in some ways and like everyone else in others. There is nothing splendid or magnificent about me.

When I remember I am a spark of the divine, I also remember that I am splendid as the divine is splendid.

The challenge is to let my essence shine through to enlighten my presence in form, so that my avatar lights up from within.

SPONTANEOUS

*B*eing spontaneous is often confused with being impulsive but that is only one interpretation of acting without thinking.

Being spontaneous is being in The Flow, being so much in tune with what I am doing that I do not need to think about what I am doing.

There are times when writing is like that, when I sit at the computer and words just come. The story tells itself and I go where the words take me and often find myself with a different plot twist to the one I had planned or a new character who has walked into the story.

But it's not magic. It comes from many hours of practice and trusting that at some level I know what I am doing. I am spontaneous when my inner critic takes a break and stops trying to dictate the words.

Watching someone who is a master at their craft or sport is an opportunity to witness spontaneous action in motion. A master makes something I think is difficult look so effortless.

It's easy to be envious until I remember the hours of training that went into developing the level of mastery required to make it look spontaneous and free flowing.

I am spontaneous also means I act without worrying about what other people think or whether they approve. It means I remember that I do not need to seek permission to be myself.

The more I let go of other people's expectations of me, the more spontaneous I allow myself to be - and that's fun.

SUCCESSFUL

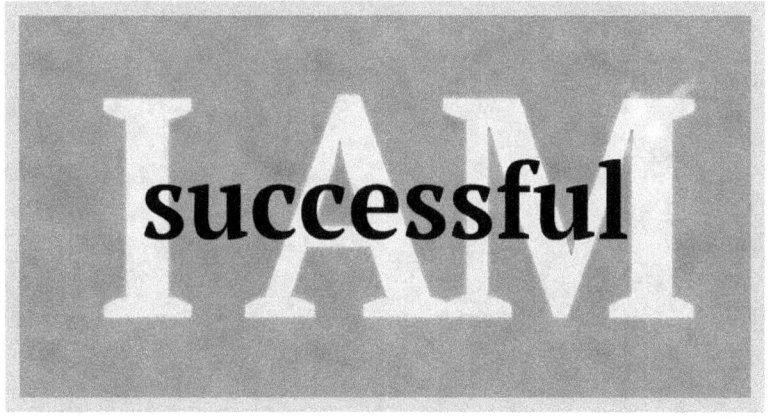

I get to define success for myself. There is no point in striving to meet someone else's definition.

I get to decide on the measures I apply to determine my success. I am not living my life to meet other people's expectations.

Life has many facets. It's not just about earning money - the world's measure of success.

I am successful in ways that have nothing to do with money and everything to do with being the type of person I choose to be in the world.

Being successful is an attitude. It's a state of mind I take with me as I walk through my day.

I get to set my own goals and measure my success in my own terms.

I believe in myself and trust the process of life - and that makes me successful.

SUPPORTIVE

Supportive people provide encouragement to others.

Sometimes, they provide actual help, but it's encouragement that works the magic.

I'm not supporting anyone when I step in and do the task for them. That's interfering.

Doing it yourself is essential for personal growth.

Doing it yourself is essential for learning.

Teaching is supportive.

Far better to teach people how to do something than to do it for them.

That way they learn they can do it when you are not around - and it's so uplifting learning to do something, anything, yourself.

Why would I want to deny that feeling to another?

Why would I deny the gift of giving to myself?

Being supportive also means being there for others when things aren't working out for them - and letting them know they are loved even when it seems they have made a mess of it.

THANKFUL

I have so much to be thankful for.

The challenge is to remember to be thankful for all of the gifts I receive each day.

I am thankful for the presence of others in my life.

I am thankful for the talents I am able to deploy in pursuit of my dreams.

I am thankful for the systems that allow me to communicate with people across the world without leaving home.

I am thankful for the field of possibilities open to me.

I am thankful for being able to change my mind and start a new adventure.

I am thankful I start each day refreshed.

I am thankful I am not trapped inside my story.

I am thankful I exist.

I am thankful for every experience. They all bring a blessing - even the ones that seem to be disasters at first.

THE LIGHT

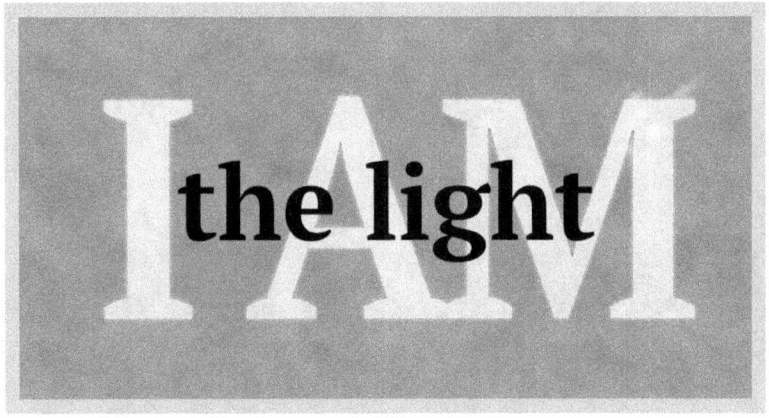

*J*esus told us we were the light of the world. He also told us not to hide our light but to let it shine for others to see. (Mathew 5:14-16 ESV).

I grew up in a culture notorious for lopping *tall poppies* or cutting people down to size. The implied message in such cultures is to conform, not to stand out.

Under such peer pressure many choose to sit in the stands and watch, instead of running into the arena and playing the game we are all here to play.

I am the light is a reminder that I am here to shine. To do that I must step into the arena and participate in the game of life.

The ego's greatest fear is not that I am small and insignificant but that I am all powerful and magnificent - and that I must let my light shine.

The ego fears my light because it will no longer be visible when I let that light shine.

That's the challenge those words of Jesus give me: stop pretending I'm a nobody and be myself in all my shining glory.

THRIVING

I am thriving.

I am flourishing.

I am doing extremely well.

I am in good health.

I am in good spirits.

I am progressing towards my goals.

I feel great.

I know I am on the right path.

I am thriving when the frequency of my vibration is aligned with Source. That's when I am not resisting. That's when I am going with the flow.

I am thriving when I give my attention to the things I want to attract into my life. That's when they appear.

I am thriving when I trust the process of life and stop trying to make things happen, when I let go and let God.

TRUSTING

I always trust people - until they demonstrate they cannot be trusted.

This means there have been times when I've discovered my trust was misplaced. Most times, though, I have found people to be trustworthy.

I trust in the process of life.

I trust that things always work for the best - even if I have to contemplate the outcome before recognizing that truth.

We take a lot of things, like beliefs and cultural norms, on trust until we are old enough to explore them for ourselves.

Some of us are so trusting, we never question what we were told by our parents or elders, and we go through life never questioning the beliefs we took on in childhood.

At some point, though, you need to trust your own understanding of life.

You need to trust your own experiences.

You need to listen to your own voice and ask your own questions, otherwise you'll never get your own answers.

VALUABLE

I am valuable. I am of value to myself and others.

I am unique and have a particular role to play in God's plan for creation - otherwise I would not exist.

I am more valuable than any priceless object.

I am always amused by the notion that something is valuable because people are prepared to pay a large amount of money to possess it.

My real value comes from being who I am and not from the tricks I perform or the functions I fulfil.

My real value comes from my willingness to share what I know and not from accumulating knowledge for my personal benefit.

My real value comes from letting my light shine.

VALUED

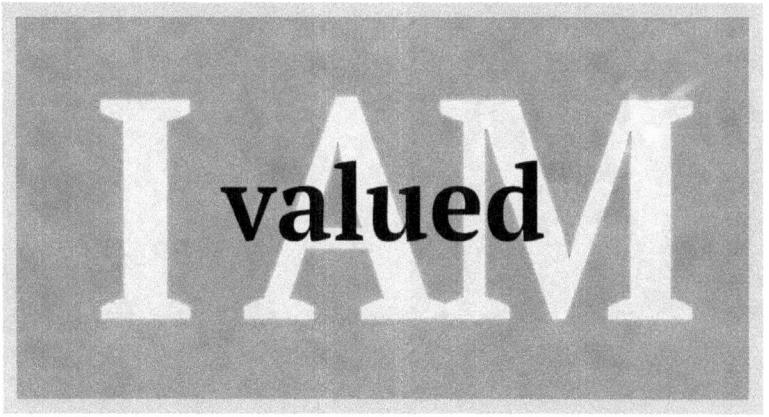

I am appreciated, cherished, and loved by people in my life.

I appreciate, cherish, and love myself.

There is nothing wrong with loving yourself. In fact, it's required.

Remember, Jesus told us to love our neighbours as we love ourselves. (Mark 12:31 ESV)

One of our greatest mistakes is refusing to love ourselves, refusing to value ourselves.

No-one is more important than you are in the eyes of God.

It doesn't matter what value the world places upon you. That's only someone's opinion.

What matters is remembering that you are appreciated, cherished, and loved by God.

VIBRANT

I am vibrant.

I am alive.

The energy of love courses through me, activating the core of my being.

I am like a beacon on a hill. My light shines brightly in all directions.

I am a centre of attention. The signal generated by my heart attracts others to me.

When I am vibrant, being with others is never draining, no matter how much energy flows from me.

When I am vibrant, I am connected to the unending flow of energy from Source.

All I have to do is let it flow through me - and remember it's not about me.

WELCOMING

I am welcoming. I allow people into my life. I do not push them away simply because they are different.

I live in a nation of immigrants and indigenous people. I am open to meeting new people, learning new things and eating different foods. I see richness in diversity and welcome it into my life experience.

I'm willing to listen to another's point of view, to hear their story and appreciate that even when we see things differently we can still be friends.

I entertain new ideas. I know that I live within a belief bubble, within a tribe or family group that has a particular worldview, but I do not want to restrict myself to that one set of beliefs. I welcome discussion and the interchange of ideas.

Being welcoming allows me to embrace the new and different and to expand my horizons.

WELL

I am well. I have a sense of well-being. This is my natural state.

I need to allow fear, worry or despair into my consciousness to lose my sense of well-being.

When my worldview was purely scientific, I believed that wellness depended on the body's immune system defending me from invasion by disease causing pathogens.

I believed that I had to eat the right foods and exercise.

I never imagined that wellness depended on what I thought or how I talked about myself.

With the integration of my scientific knowledge with my spiritual knowing, I now appreciate that my wellness also depends on my state of mind and my thoughts and beliefs.

This is actually quite a powerful insight, as it means I can exercise control of my wellness and not leave it to what's blowing in the wind. And, at those times when I succumb to a disease causing pathogen, I am able to direct my thoughts to regaining my wellness.

It's sobering to think that science has known this for as long as scientists have been testing new medicines against placebos.

Funny how I didn't make the connection when I was looking down microscopes.

WILLING

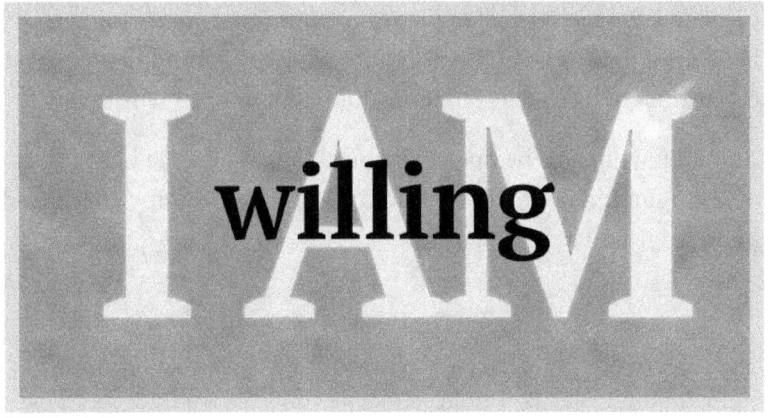

This might be the most useful of these affirmations.

It's certainly one of the most powerful because being willing opens doors to possibilities.

Being willing allows me to consider the possibility that what I want to believe about myself may be the truth.

If I'm not willing to entertain the thought that I can use I am affirmations as a self-awareness tool, I may as well not make those statements.

If I'm not willing to examine, and maybe change, my beliefs about myself and how the universe operates, I will stay within the world I've created unconsciously by mindlessly repeating other people's beliefs.

I am choosing not to stay there; it's not a safe place.

I am open. This affirmation is a challenge for a mind educated in the scientific method, for a mind that wants to see the proof, the evidence. It's really challenging for a mind that wants to be right, for a mind that is an authority in its field, for a mind that believes the argument has been settled in alignment with its worldview.

But, I am willing to be open is a portal that allows the light of new ideas to illuminate the dark spaces in the library of my confirmed knowledge and beliefs.

I am divine. That is a huge concept to allow and accept. That's imagining I am like God.

But, I am willing to be divine lets me open my mind to exploring what that means, what that feels like, and that's not so scary. That's a journey of discovery I can go on.

I am one with Source. It's taken me years of meditation to become aware of being one with Source and to open to accepting the reality of that dimension of existence. That's a big leap in faith to achieve through an affirmation.

But, I am willing to be one with Source is another pathway to that truth. It's a first step on the journey.

I am willing is a belief bubble buster.

I am willing is an affirmation that allows me to expand the scope of my understanding of who I am and what I'm capable of achieving in this world.

A NOTE FROM PETER

If you enjoyed **Beyond the Words: Reflections on I Am Affirmations** you can help other readers share your enjoyment by telling them about the book and writing a review.

If you're interested in reading the thoughts of a modern-day mystic, visit www.petermulraney.com, where you can subscribe to my monthly newsletter 'Insights from a crime writing mystic' and download a free copy of *A Question of Perspective*.

Thank you for buying the book.

Peter Mulraney

Drop by and say hello.
www.petermulraney.com
peter@petermulraney.com

ALSO BY PETER MULRANEY

Writings of the Mystic

Sharing the Journey: Reflections of a Reluctant Mystic

A Question of Perspective (Paperback)

My Life is My Responsibility: Insights for Conscious Living

I Am Affirmations: The Power of Words

Mystical Journey: A Handbook for Modern Mystics

Sharing the Journey Coloring Books

Mandalas

Mandalas by 3

Sharing the Journey Coloring Journals

Sharing the Journey Coloring Journal

Sharing the Journey Coloring Journal ~Discovery

Sharing the Journey Coloring Journal ~ Reflection

Crime fiction and self-help

Peter Mulraney also writes crime fiction and self-help. You can sample all of his books in his free Official Reading Guide.

www.ingramcontent.com/pod-product-compliance
Lightning Source LLC
Chambersburg PA
CBHW071925290426
44110CB00013B/1476